# TRUE OR FALSE?

↰ This amazing photo shows the Loch Ness Monster chasing a man in a kayak.

# FALSE!

The picture was made in Photoshop, a computer program that makes it easy to create fake photos. A Photoshop artist combined these photos into one image.

All over the world, there are people who claim that they've spotted monsters — and that they have the photos to prove it. Are these photos real? Do the creatures in them actually exist? As you'll see in this book, sometimes it's hard to tell.

Book design Red Herring Design/NYC
Supervising editor: Jeffrey Nelson

Library of Congress Cataloging-in-Publication Data
Teitelbaum, Michael, 1953–
Bigfoot caught on film : and other monster sightings! /
By Michael Teitelbaum
p. cm. – (24/7: science behind the scenes)
Includes bibliographical references and index.
ISBN-13: 978-0-531-12078-1 (lib. bdg.)   978-0-531-17531-6 (pbk.)
ISBN-10: 0-531-12078-3 (lib. bdg.)   0-531-17531-6 (pbk.)
1. Sasquatch—Juvenile literature. 2. Yeti—Juvenile literature. I. Title.
QL89.2S2T42 2008
001.944—dc22   2006021236

# BIGFOOT
# CAUGHT
# ON FILM

## And Other
## Monster Sightings!

Michael Teitelbaum

**WARNING:** **If you're horrified by the idea that a hairy giant with terrible body odor might be roaming the woods—YOU'VE PICKED UP THE WRONG BOOK!**

**Franklin Watts**
An Imprint of Scholastic Inc.
New York • Toronto • London • Auckland • Sydney
Mexico City • New Delhi • Hong Kong
Danbury, Connecticut

# CONTENTS

## CRYPTID 411

What's cryptozoology?
Find out in this section—
and meet some monsters.

# TRUE-LIFE CASE FILES!

Follow the investigators trying to find Earth's most mysterious creatures.

Is this Bigfoot? Or is it a man in a gorilla suit?

**15 Case #1:**
## The Case of the Missing Body
There have been hundreds of Bigfoot sightings. So why hasn't anyone found a body— or at least some bones?

**Case #2:**
## Searching for Nessie
**27**
Is there a monster in Loch Ness? Or does it exist only in people's imaginations?

This photo made the Loch Ness Monster famous. Was it real?

**37 Case #3:**
## A Real Monster
This sea creature has eyes the size of a human head. For real.

How did this man manage to film a giant squid?

Track down some mysterious beasts, and meet the researchers who study them.

"Do you believe in Bigfoot?"

Every culture has stories of strange and wonderful creatures. Most of them exist only in myths and legends.

## CRYPTID 411

But do some of them actually roam the earth? Cryptozoologists think so. These researchers look for evidence of mysterious animals whose existence has not yet been proven.

### IN THIS SECTION:

▶ words you need to know, like "crittercam" and "cryptid";

▶ all about the bloodsucking Chupacabra;

▶ and what looks like an ape but smells like a skunk?

# Can You Believe It?

Look at this photo! Do you need more evidence that the skunk ape is real?

**evidence**
(EV-uh-denss) information and objects that help people make judgments or come to conclusions

**cryptid**
(KRIP-tid) a creature that some people believe is real but whose existence has not been scientifically proven

But people have reported sightings of this cryptid all over the state.

Are you always such a skeptic?

**skeptic**
(SKEP-tik) someone who questions ideas or beliefs

## hoax

(hohks) an act or trick designed to fool people into believing something that isn't true

## cryptozoology

(KRIP-toh-zoh-OL-uh-jee) the study of hidden, unknown, or yet-to-be-discovered animals

That's a guy in a gorilla suit. The skunk ape is a big hoax. These fakes threaten to make a joke out of cryptozoology.

What makes you think those people are credible? They might be imagining things—or lying!

## credible

(KRED-uh-buhl) believable; capable of being believed

# Say What?

**Here's more monster lingo.**

## crittercams

(KRIT-ur-kamz) video cameras that researchers attach to animals. Crittercams let people see an animal's world from its point of view.
*"The squid hunters hoped that the whales with **crittercams** would encounter some giant squid."*

## mythical creature

(MITH-i-kuhl KREE-chur) a fantastic animal that exists only in legends and folktales
*"Unicorns are **mythical creatures**."*

## urban myth

(UR-buhn mith) a strangely believable but untrue story that many people believe. Like rumors, urban myths spread fast.
*"One **urban myth** is that insects called earwigs crawl into your ear and eat their way through your brain."*

# The Cryptid Files

**People swear they've seen these creatures with their own eyes. But have they?**

This illustration of a Chupacabra is based on eyewitness descriptions.

You may already know a few cryptids. In fact, some of these creatures are pretty famous—even though their existence has never been proven.

There's Bigfoot, for example. That's the name of the ape-like creatures that have been spotted all over North America. And there's the Loch Ness Monster. Supposedly, it lives in a lake in Scotland.

But what about the Chupacabra? Or the Mothman? Here's some information about them and some other cryptids. Keep in mind that no bones or bodies of any of these creatures have ever been found . . .

## Chupacabra (or "Goatsucker")

**AREA:** The Americas

**FIRST SIGHTING:** Puerto Rico in the early 1990s

**EVIDENCE FOR:** Locals reported **sightings** of a strange creature, as well as the mysterious deaths of farm animals. People believed that a mysterious **predator** was killing the animals and sucking their blood.

**EVIDENCE AGAINST:** Tests in Puerto Rico by the National Geographic Channel showed that the animals had been killed by other animals or by people.

## Ogopogo

A photo of Ogopogo—but it's probably a fake.

**AREA:** Okanagan Lake, British Columbia, Canada

**FIRST SIGHTING:** There are Native Canadian **legends** about a great lake serpent. People offered it **sacrifices** so they could cross the lake safely.

**EVIDENCE FOR:** There have been many eyewitness reports, including some by groups of people who said they saw Ogopogo at the same time.

**EVIDENCE AGAINST:** The monster in legends was fierce and evil. Modern eyewitnesses describe the one they've seen as playful. Real animals' behavior doesn't change over time.

An artist's representation of Mothman.

## Mothman

**AREA:** Point Pleasant, West Virginia

**FIRST SIGHTING:** November 12, 1966

**EVIDENCE FOR:** Several hundred people reported seeing or being chased by a tall, winged creature with glowing red eyes.

**EVIDENCE AGAINST:** The sightings stopped suddenly after a year. Many skeptics thought that the eyewitnesses had just seen large birds such as cranes—or that the whole thing was a hoax.

This Florida Skunk Ape was supposedly spotted in a couple's backyard near Sarasota, Florida, in 2000.

## Florida Skunk Ape

**AREA:** Southeastern U.S.

**FIRST SIGHTING:** Occasional sightings have been reported for 200 years. There have been about 75 sightings in the past 20 years.

**EVIDENCE FOR:** The best evidence is two photos taken by an elderly Florida couple in 2000. They said that they saw (and smelled!) an ape-like animal in their backyard. **Cryptozoologists** think it might have been a skunk ape, an undiscovered animal known for its terrible odor.

**EVIDENCE AGAINST:** Many of the reported sightings were in the Big Cypress Swamp in Florida. So it's strange that the park rangers who work there have never seen one. Most rangers think the skunk ape is probably a hoax.

## Mokèlé-Mbèmbé

**AREA:** Cameroon and Republic of Congo, Africa

**FIRST SIGHTING:** For more than 200 years, residents have been telling visitors about a swamp-dwelling, dinosaur-like creature they called Mokèlé-Mbèmbé.

**EVIDENCE FOR:** Several teams have gone on **expeditions** to search for this living dinosaur. All heard stories by local people who said they'd seen the animal. Some teams reported finding large and mysterious footprints. A few team members claimed they'd seen or heard the animal.

**EVIDENCE AGAINST:** There are no clear photographs or videos of this cryptid.

This painting of the Mokèlé-Mbèmbé from Cameroon and Congo is based on descriptions by eyewitnesses.

12

# TRUE-LIFE CASE FILES!

**Many people believe that there are giant, unknown creatures living in the world's forests, lakes, and oceans. And cryptozoologists are working 24/7 to find them.**

IN THIS SECTION:

how hoaxes have complicated the search for Bigfoot;

why most researchers think the search for the Loch Ness Monster is over;

how scientists finally managed to get photos of a legendary deep-sea monster.

# Tracking Monsters

## How do you know if a cryptid has walked by recently?

Say you're a cryptozoologist. How do you prove that you've found a cryptid?

You need evidence. If you're really lucky, you'll get a photo or video.

Another kind of evidence is footprints. It's every cryptozoologist's dream to find a strange set of footprints in an area where a creature has been spotted.

### Casts of Footprints

If you find some footprints, here's what you do next.

▶ Take photos. Put a ruler next to each print to show the size. If you don't have a ruler, use something with a standard size—like a soda can.

▶ Make a sketch to show how many footprints are there. Number each footprint.

▶ If there are several prints, measure the stride. What's the distance from the tip of one right foot to another?

▶ Make a **plaster cast** of each footprint. To do that, carefully pour wet plaster into the print. Allow it to partially harden. Then write the date, time, and location on it. Also write the number you gave this print on your sketch.

Does all this mean that you should believe every cryptid photo and footprint that you see? Of course not. They can easily be faked!

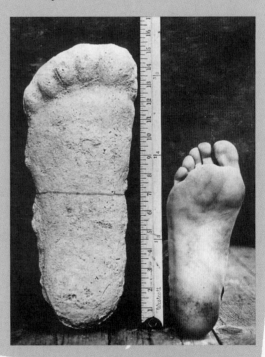

Cryptozoologists claim that the cast on the left is the footprint of a Bigfoot. It was made in 1967, just after a Bigfoot was supposedly caught on film.

North America
1958-present

## The Case of the Missing Body

**There have been hundreds of Bigfoot sightings. So why hasn't anyone found a body— or at least some bones?**

# Bigfoot Is Born

**Giant footprints are found deep in the forest, and the Bigfoot story begins.**

One morning in August 1958, Jerry Crew arrived at his work site. He was part of a crew cutting logging roads through the woods of northern California. As he walked toward his bulldozer, he noticed something strange. There were huge footprints in the newly dug road. They looked like human footprints, only much bigger.

New footprints continued to appear at the site. After a few weeks, Crew decided to make plaster casts of the prints.

People were amazed when they saw the casts. The footprints were 16 inches (41 cm) long and seven inches (18 cm) wide! No known animal in the area had feet that big. What kind of creature had made the prints? The local paper gave the beast a name that stuck: Bigfoot.

Other papers picked up the story. Soon people all over the country had heard about the creature with triple-wide size 16 feet. The legend of Bigfoot was born.

*Jerry Crew shows off the plaster cast he made of a giant footprint he found in the forest. Papers all over the country picked up his story.*

Huge Footprints Found On Wilderness Road

# Wildmen of the World

**Bigfoot is not alone. Many other cultures have legends about similar creatures.**

Native American legends tell of a Bigfoot-like beast living in the woods. It was said to be bigger and stronger than a bear. Some tribes called it Windigo. Others knew it as Sasquatch. Both names mean "wild man of the woods."

Descriptions of similar creatures are found in reports by early settlers in North America. And many other cultures have stories of a giant man-ape. In Nepal and Tibet, it's known as the Yeti. In Australia, it's called Yowie. And there are Chinese folktales about a wildman called the Yeren.

Climber Eric Shipton took this photo while climbing Mount Everest in 1951. The footprint was 13 inches (33 cm) long. Some people see it as evidence that the Yeti exists.

After Jerry Crew spotted the footprints in northern California, people began searching for Bigfoot. One of the first researchers was Roger Patterson. In 1966, he wrote a book called *Do Abominable Snowmen of America Really Exist?* The legends about such creatures, along with reported sightings, convinced him that the answer was yes.

Patterson knew that it wouldn't be enough to find footprints. To prove its existence, he would have to capture Bigfoot on film. So he raised some money to rent a camera and make a film. Then he set out to find the hairy beast.

# Bigfoot Caught! (On Film)

**A short film clip from 1967 is still considered the best evidence of Bigfoot's existence.**

Here's a frame from the film Roger Patterson made in 1967. He spotted this creature near a creek in northern California. Researchers concluded that it was a female Bigfoot.

In October 1967, Roger Patterson and a friend, Bob Gimlin, set out on their expedition. They decided to explore an area near where Crew had found the footprints. They were riding on horseback along a mountain trail when they saw a tall, shaggy creature drinking from the stream.

The horses were spooked by the sight and reared up. The creature noticed them and began moving away. Patterson grabbed his movie camera. He managed to shoot less than a minute of film before the creature disappeared into the woods. But he had what he'd come for.

The film showed a large ape-like animal with a long stride. Researchers who went back to the site found a few big footprints. Based on the film and the footprints, they figured that the creature was close to seven feet (2 m) tall and weighed 300 to 800 pounds (136 to 363 kg).

Or was it just a very big hoax? Many people thought so. But Patterson said that he hadn't faked anything. And after studying the film, most Bigfoot researchers concluded that it was real. They saw it as proof that Bigfoot existed.

**Say Bigfoot exists. What could it possibly be?**

Cryptozoologists think that Bigfoot must be a kind of ape. One of the first and most respected Bigfoot researchers was Dr. Grover Krantz. His theory was that Bigfoot was the living ancestor of an extinct ape called *Gigantopithecus blacki*.

Researchers estimate that there are a few thousand Bigfoots alive today. They describe the creature as shy. They also say that it's nocturnal—it only comes out at night. Maybe that's why it's so hard to find!

# Fact or Fiction?

**Cryptozoologists say there is plenty of evidence that Bigfoot exists. Skeptics disagree.**

In the 40 years since Roger Patterson made his film, people have gathered evidence of the monster's existence. Thousands of Bigfoot sightings have been reported. Some people have managed to take pictures of the beast, but most of the images are blurry. Other trackers have recorded sounds they claim were made by a Bigfoot. And researchers have collected lots of footprints and some hair samples.

This is an artist's impression of what Bigfoot might look like.

Some observers even claim they've caught a whiff of Bigfoot. They say the big guy smells nasty.

But is any of this evidence real? Pranksters have admitted to creating a lot of it. For example, some of these jokers confess that they've strapped on big wooden feet and stomped around to make Bigfoot tracks.

One skeptic, a writer named Benjamin Radford, took a close look at a lot of the evidence. He concluded that none of it was credible. All Bigfoot samples have been found "to be hoaxes, **inconclusive**, or from known animals," he writes.

Bigfoot researchers think that Radford looked at only some of the evidence. They admit that there have been many hoaxes. But they say that there is still plenty of good evidence to support their belief in Bigfoot. And a few scientists agree with them.

So who is more credible—the skeptics or the believers? To decide for yourself, examine the evidence closely.

## Does Patterson's film show a real Bigfoot—or a person in a gorilla suit?

**Believers:** People who think Bigfoot exists say that the creature couldn't be a person in a gorilla suit. The chest is too big. The arms are too long. It doesn't walk the way humans do. And some Hollywood special effects experts have said that they couldn't create a fake animal that looks and moves like the one in the film.

**Skeptics:** The doubters find it suspicious that Patterson set out to film a Bigfoot—and succeeded on his first try! They also think it's strange that no other Bigfoot has been spotted in that area since the film was made. And they point out that a few years ago, a man named Bob Heironimus claimed that Patterson hired him to wear a gorilla suit. Another man, Philip Morris, said that he made the suit.

Is this a picture of a man named Bob Heironimus in a gorilla suit? He claims it is. In 2004, Heironimus revealed that he was Bigfoot in Patterson's film. "I think after 35 years, the truth should come out," he said. He added that when he was dressed as Bigfoot he worried that a hunter would shoot him.

## Are the Bigfoot footprints solid evidence?

**Believers:** Cryptozoologists say that no known animal could have made the footprints. Some experts even say that humans wearing fake feet couldn't have made them. And so many prints have been found that it's unlikely that pranksters are responsible for all of them.

Professor Jeffrey Meldrum teaches **anatomy** and **anthropology** at Idaho Sate University. He studies the way humans and **primates** walk. Meldrum has collected and examined many Bigfoot footprints. In an interview with *National Geographic*, he said: "Given the scientific evidence I've examined, I'm convinced that there's a creature out there that is yet to be identified."

Shown here are plaster casts of footprints said to belong to Bigfoot. In 2006, a museum in Idaho included them in an exhibit about Bigfoot.

**Skeptics:** They say that the footprints are too different for one animal to have made them. They were probably made by many different pranksters.

## Are eyewitness accounts believable?

**Believers:** Bigfoot researchers agree that some reported sightings are hoaxes. But they say that the thousands of people who claim to have seen a Bigfoot can't all be lying, mistaken, or crazy.

**Skeptics:** Eyewitness accounts are often unreliable. For example, somebody in an area considered "Bigfoot country" might see a bear in the distance and decide it's a Bigfoot. It's called wishful thinking. You see what you want to see.

## A last word from both sides . . .

**Believers:** They point out that people also thought that the African mountain gorilla was a myth. Then, after a hunter killed one in 1902, the myth became reality. They think something similar will happen with Bigfoot.

**Skeptics:** They say that the biggest reason to doubt Bigfoot's existence is that no body or skeleton has ever been found.

# The Death of Bigfoot?

## The family of a dead man claims that he made the footprints that Jerry Crew discovered in 1958.

In 2002, the press reported a shocking story. The family of a man named Ray Wallace was claiming that he had made the huge footprints discovered by Jerry Crew almost 50 years earlier.

Wallace owned the construction company that Jerry Crew worked for in 1958. He was known as a practical joker. And he had bragged that he had used wooden "track stompers" to make the footprints that had fooled Jerry Crew decades before.

When Wallace died in 2002, the family told his story, and it made headlines around the country. Crew's discovery of the footprints had started the Bigfoot craze. Many people saw Wallace's story as proof that Bigfoot doesn't exist.

But Bigfoot researchers laughed. They said that Wallace's claim that he was "the father of Bigfoot" was just a final hoax. And they said that his stompers didn't even match the tracks that Crew found.

What's your opinion? Do you side with the scientists who say that there is no solid evidence that an undiscovered ape **species**

Ray Wallace's nephew, Dale Lee Wallace, shows off the carved feet that he says were used to make Bigfoot's footprints.

exists in North America? Or do you agree with those who say that the sightings suggest that Bigfoot really exists?

One highly respected scientist surprised everyone with her opinion. Jane Goodall is famous for her discoveries about **chimpanzees**. In 2003, she told an interviewer that she was sure that Bigfoot exists. But by the end of the interview, Goodall sounded less certain. "Maybe they don't exist, but I want them to," she said.

Her spokesperson later clarified Goodall's position: "As a scientist, she's very curious and she keeps an open mind," the spokesperson said. "She's fascinated by [the question]."

So are many other people. But unless somebody catches a Bigfoot, or a body or skeleton is found, most scientists will remain skeptical. 24/7

Jane Goodall is famous for her discoveries about chimps. She is keeping an open mind about Bigfoot.

# HAIRY ENCOUNTERS
## Have you seen a Bigfoot recently?

There is serious doubt among many experts that a hairy giant lives in North America. But people keep seeing *something* strange in the woods. Quite a few sightings are reported every year.

The Bigfoot Field Researchers Organization (BFRO) wants to find solid evidence that the species exists. Some of its members go on expeditions to search for Bigfoot. And the group keeps track of all reported sightings.

According to information gathered by BFRO, Hawaii is the only state with no sightings. But as you know, sightings only prove that people saw something they can't explain.

## Reported Bigfoot Sightings in the U.S. (since the 1950s)

| | | | | | |
|---|---|---|---|---|---|
| Alabama | 42 | Louisiana | 32 | Ohio | 191 |
| Alaska | 19 | Maine | 13 | Oklahoma | 62 |
| Arizona | 40 | Maryland | 25 | Oregon | 199 |
| Arkansas | 64 | Massachusetts | 10 | Pennsylvania | 78 |
| California | 363 | Michigan | 73 | Rhode Island | 3 |
| Colorado | 85 | Minnesota | 32 | South Carolina | 35 |
| Connecticut | 4 | Mississippi | 18 | South Dakota | 13 |
| Delaware | 2 | Missouri | 54 | Tennessee | 51 |
| Florida | 117 | Montana | 24 | Texas | 160 |
| Georgia | 48 | Nebraska | 7 | Utah | 42 |
| Hawaii | 0 | Nevada | 7 | Vermont | 6 |
| Idaho | 50 | New Hampshire | 9 | Virginia | 23 |
| Illinois | 59 | New Jersey | 39 | Washington | 411 |
| Indiana | 49 | New Mexico | 32 | West Virginia | 47 |
| Iowa | 35 | New York | 86 | Wisconsin | 42 |
| Kansas | 26 | North Carolina | 49 | Wyoming | 24 |
| Kentucky | 47 | North Dakota | 5 | | |

Source: BFRO

In the next case, find out about the search for the famous Loch Ness Monster.

Loch Ness, Scotland
1930s-present

# Searching for Nessie

Is there a monster in Loch Ness?
Or does it exist only in
people's imagination?

# "A Strange Spectacle"

## A couple sees an enormous animal in a lake. The local paper names it the Loch Ness Monster.

It was a clear spring day in 1933, and John and Aldie Mackay were out for a drive. They were on a road that had recently been built along Loch Ness, the biggest lake in Scotland. Trees had been cut down when the road was built, and the Mackays could see the lake stretching for miles.

Suddenly, Mrs. Mackay saw a dark shape moving through the water. At first she thought it was ducks splashing. But then she saw a huge hump rising out of the water. She grabbed her husband's arm and pointed. They watched "the **enormous** animal rolling and plunging on the surface," as they said later. After a few moments, it disappeared into the dark lake.

The Mackays were stunned. The creature looked like a whale. But they knew there were no whales in Loch Ness. What could it be?

At first, the Mackays worried that people would think they were crazy if they told them what they'd seen. But soon they began telling friends, and the story spread.

Some people laughed at their story. But others believed them. After all, they'd all heard the old legends about a monster that lived in the lake. Maybe the creature was more than a myth.

A local paper printed a story about the Mackays' sighting. And over the next few weeks,

Loch Ness is in the mountains of Scotland. Today, the area's rugged beauty attracts millions of tourists. They come to admire the scenery and the old castles. They also come to see if they can catch a glimpse of the monster that made the lake famous.

In the spring of 1933, John and Aldie Mackay were driving along Loch Ness, the biggest lake in Scotland. Suddenly, they saw a huge creature in the water, but it soon disappeared. What could it have been?

SCOTLAND

EUROPE

This article from the *Inverness Courier*, a Scottish newspaper, described the Mackays' sighting. The reporters called the creature the "Loch Ness Monster." That's been its name ever since.

more people claimed to have seen the creature.

"It was big as an elephant," reported a farmer. "It looked right at me," said a visiting businessman.

Suddenly, the Loch Ness Monster was big news. But the story was just beginning.

# A Monster Story

**The first photos appear, and the creature becomes famous around the world.**

A year after the Mackays' sighting, a doctor from London named Robert K. Wilson visited Loch Ness. He told people later that he and a friend were driving along the shore when they saw a strange creature in the water.

Wilson grabbed his camera and started shooting. One of his photos showed a large, long-necked animal swimming in the middle of the lake. He sold the photo to an English newspaper. Soon it appeared in papers around the world.

The photo caused a sensation. People began coming to Loch Ness to look for the monster. And more and more people reported seeing it. But only a few managed to take pictures, and most of those were blurry.

The people who said they'd seen Nessie, as the

monster was often called, described it in detail. Some said that it was a serpent-like creature with one or more humps on its back. Others described it as having a long, thin neck.

A few people even said they chased the monster so they could get a better look at it.

One of them was Hugh Ayton. He and his son were working in his fields when they saw something big in the lake. It was moving silently through the water.

Ayton, his son, and two other men jumped into a boat and followed the beast. Ayton said it was 30 to 40 feet (9 to 12 m) long and had three small humps. "There was a long neck coming about 6 feet (2 m) out of the water," he said.

When they got near the creature, it dove underwater. But then it rose up again. It had "an oval-shaped eye near the top of its head," Ayton said. "I'll always remember that eye looking at us."

There were many other accounts that sounded as convincing as Ayton's. So you'd think it would have been easy for investigators to find proof of Nessie's existence. But it wasn't.

In 1934, a doctor named Robert K. Wilson said that he saw the Loch Ness monster and took this photo. It made the creature famous.

# The Searchers

**Researchers have spent years looking for evidence that Nessie exists. They haven't found much.**

One of the most **determined** investigators was Tim Dinsdale. In 1960, this British engineer decided that all the eyewitness accounts couldn't be wrong. So he set out to capture Nessie on film. On his fifth day at the lake, he got lucky.

Dinsdale shot four minutes of film of something moving in the lake. The film was analyzed by photographic experts. They concluded that what he'd filmed was "probably alive." The people who believed in Nessie celebrated. They were sure that they now had proof that the monster was real.

Dinsdale spent 27 years searching for the monster. But he never caught the Loch Ness Monster on film again.

In 1962, a group called the Loch Ness Investigation Bureau began its search for Nessie. Some researchers set up permanent camera stations at several places around the lake. They also had vans with cameras mounted on top. Other researchers used submarines and listening devices to search underwater. But in ten years of operation, the

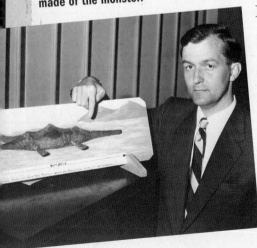

Engineer Tim Dinsdale claimed to have caught Nessie on film. But when experts re-examined the film in the 1990s, they decided that the object he had filmed was probably a fishing boat. Here, Dinsdale displays a model he made of the monster.

group found few signs of a large creature living in the lake.

In 1987, Operation Deepscan used **sonar** equipment (see box below) to scan the lake. TV crews from around the world covered the event. The team recorded three large objects they could not explain. But in the end, no big discoveries were made.

In 2003, another team used sonar to scan the entire lake from "shoreline to shoreline, top to bottom." They found logs and old buoys. "We found no signs of any large living animal," said scientist Ian Florence. "I think this might settle the question. There is nothing there."

In 1969, researchers used a submarine called *Viperfish* to search for Nessie.

# SEEING WITH SOUND
## Scientists use sonar to search for Nessie.

Cameras aren't much good in a place as deep and dark as Loch Ness. So scientists often use sonar equipment instead. Sonar uses sound waves to capture images underwater. The equipment sends out sound pulses. Then it measures how long it takes for the pulses to bounce off objects and return. A computer translates that information into images of the objects.

# What Could Nessie Be?

## If the monster does exist, what kind of animal is it?

Researchers have come up with different theories about what kind of animal the monster could be. Here are some of the most popular ones.

**Is the Loch Ness Monster a plesiosaur? These ancient reptiles had long necks and flippers and lived in water.**

### An Ancient Reptile

In 1975, American researcher Robert Rines used an underwater camera in Loch Ness. One of his photos was blurry but seemed to show a large flipper. Some experts then concluded that Nessie was a plesiosaur, a reptile that lived in the time of dinosaurs.

But many scientists questioned this theory. After all, plesiosaurs died out millions of years ago. And even if some had survived, how could they live in a cold lake? Plesiosaurs were warm-water reptiles.

### A Monster Mammal

Some people have suggested that Nessie could be a marine **mammal** similar to a whale. But mammals breathe air. If Nessie was a mammal, it would have to rise to the surface to breathe. That means it would be seen much more often.

Also, large mammals need lots of food. Loch Ness is cold and dark. There aren't enough fish and plants to feed a big animal.

## A Gigantic Fish

Or maybe Nessie is an enormous sturgeon. A sturgeon can weigh up to 1,000 pounds (454 kg), and it has a small fin on its back. When it's time to lay eggs, some sturgeons swim up rivers to freshwater lakes. So it's possible that a giant sturgeon has been migrating to Loch Ness. But if that were the case, people would have seen it swimming up the river that leads to the lake. That hasn't happened.

This huge sturgeon was caught in a lake in Washington State. It was 11 feet (3 m).

# End of Story?

**A classic photo turns out to be a hoax.**

Remember the famous photo taken by Dr. Wilson in 1934? It made people around the world believe in the Loch Ness Monster. Sixty years later, a man named Christian Spurling admitted that the photo was a fake. He had built the creature that was used in the photo. It was a toy model only a foot (0.3 m) high.

Many other classic photos of Nessie also turned out to be hoaxes. And researchers who

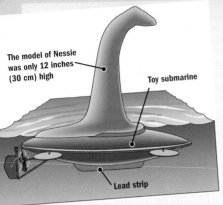

The model of Nessie was only 12 inches (30 cm) high

Toy submarine

Lead strip

According to this diagram, the monster in the 1934 photo was a toy submarine with a long neck and head attached.

spent decades watching the lake found little evidence that Nessie really exists.

But what about the thousands of people who claim they saw Nessie? Some were **fibbing**, of course. Others probably mistook other things—logs, overturned boats, groups of ducks, even swimming deer—for the monster.

Scientists have offered another possible explanation. Loch Ness has powerful underwater **currents** that create unusual waves on the surface. And small earthquakes under the lake also cause big waves. Those waves could look like strange shapes in the water.

Here's one last thing to think about. Scientists estimate that there would have to be at least 10–20 Nessies in order for the species to breed and survive. If there were that many monsters swimming around, wouldn't people be seeing them all the time?

So is the story over? Most scientists see no point in continuing to search for Nessie. But people still visit Loch Ness in hopes of seeing the monster. You never know . . . **24/7**

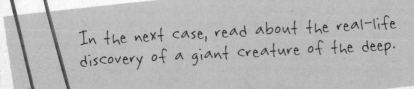

In the next case, read about the real-life discovery of a giant creature of the deep.

The world's oceans
12th century–present

# A Real Monster

This sea creature has eyes the
size of a human head.
For real.

# On the Back of a Giant

**For hundreds of years, sailors told tales about a giant sea monster known as the kraken.**

The man stands at the front of the boat, staring ahead. He looks surprised. There's an island just ahead. But there are no islands marked on his map. He must have discovered a new one.

The man goes ashore to celebrate his discovery. Then he and his crew row away. He turns for a last look and is stunned by what he sees. The island is sinking. After a moment, it vanishes beneath the waves.

Suddenly the man realizes what happened. He'd been standing on the back of a gigantic sea monster known as the kraken.

That story is from the country of Norway. It dates back to the 12th century. There are many

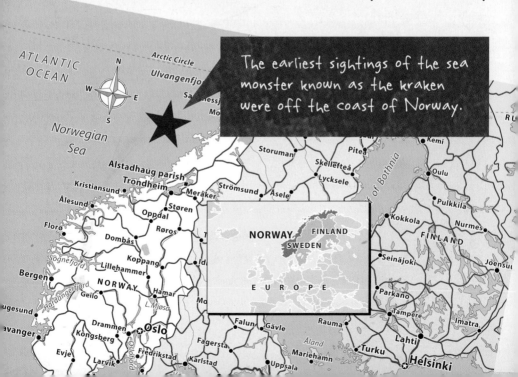

The earliest sightings of the sea monster known as the kraken were off the coast of Norway.

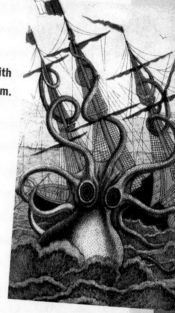

Sailors claimed that a kraken could pull ships underwater with its strong arms—and crush them.

other tales about the kraken. And the creature is often described as being as big as an island. People said that when the creature dove underwater, it created a whirlpool that swallowed up all nearby boats.

Later accounts of the kraken were a little more believable. In 1734, a missionary named Hans Egede described it this way: "A sea-monster appeared to us, whose head . . . was on level with [the top of our mast]."

Was the missionary describing a real animal? Or was the kraken a creature of myth?

# A Sea of Monsters

**Of all the legendary sea monsters, only one turned out to be real.**

For thousands of years, people believed that the seas were filled with monsters. The kraken was one of the strangest ones. But sailors also told tales of giant sea serpents and fantastic sea dragons. They reported seeing mermaids and fish with human heads.

In modern times, the invention of underwater cameras gave scientists a clearer view of the ocean. They saw that many strange creatures

FABVLOSO EQVO NE??
FALSO QVIBVSDAM HIPPOCAMPVM ET HIPPO-
potamum appellare libuit, Bellonius.

Among the weirdest
sea monsters were
the hippocampus (*top
right*) and the sea
monk (*above*). These
pictures are from
natural history books
printed in the late
1500s.

lived there, but sea dragons weren't among them. And neither were mermaids.

But they did find the kraken. Or at least, they found an animal similar to the legendary sea monster. It was identified as the giant squid. This is the story of how scientists discovered it—and how, after many setbacks, they finally managed to film it.

# A Big-Eyed Giant

## Scientists identify an odd new species.

In 1857, the kraken got a new name. Fishermen gave a Danish **zoologist** named Japetus Steenstrup pieces of what they said was a sea monster. Steenstrup recognized that it was actually a type of squid. Since then, it's been called the giant squid.

Many scientists didn't believe that such a creature existed. But that began to change in the 1870s, when more pieces of the beast turned up.

On an October morning in 1873, three men were fishing near the coast of Newfoundland. Suddenly, an immense creature rose from the sea and wrapped its **tentacles** around their boat. Its

beak-like mouth was wide open, as if it meant to devour them.

One of the men grabbed an axe and chopped off a tentacle. The beast let go and sank back into the water. But part of the tentacle still clung to the boat. The fishermen brought it back to shore. The piece was 19 feet (6 m) long. A scientist estimated that the whole animal must have been close to 60 feet (18 m) long.

In 1874, fishermen found the first whole giant squid. It was displayed in the bathtub of a man named Moses Harvey.

A year later, local fishermen found a whole specimen. They sold it to Reverend Moses Harvey, who displayed it for the public. Then the squid was sent to professor A. E. Verrill at Yale University. He conducted the first-ever scientific study of an entire giant squid.

In 1877, another whole squid was found in Newfoundland. It was described as "nearly perfect" and was also sent to Verrill for study. Now there was no longer any doubt that the giant squid was a real animal.

Verrill received many specimens over the years, but he was never able to study the largest one ever found in his lifetime. It washed up on a Newfoundland beach in 1878. Fishermen

This is an illustration of the giant squid found in Newfoundland in 1877. It was still alive when it washed ashore but died a little while later.

measured the beast. Its body was 20 feet (6 m) long, and one tentacle stretched for another 35 feet (11 m)!

But it was the eyes that really shocked the men. Each was the size of a human head.

Several witnesses confirmed these measurements. But Verrill never saw the squid with his own eyes. Unfortunately, the fishermen cut up the huge squid to use as dog food.

# IT'S SPINELESS
**The giant squid is the biggest animal of its kind on Earth.**

The giant squid is an **invertebrate**. That means that it doesn't have a spine—what you might call a backbone. In fact, it's the biggest invertebrate on Earth. The largest giant squid ever found was 59 feet (18 m) long. But scientists think that this animal can grow even bigger than that.

What else do you need to know about the giant squid? It has eight powerful arms with suckers on them, and two longer tentacles that it uses to feed itself. The giant squid eats fish and smaller squid. Its eyes are the biggest in the animal kingdom.

# Wanted: A Live Giant Squid

**Scientists had only specimens of dead giant squids to study. One man set out to change that.**

Verrill and other scientists fascinated by the giant squid never got to study a live specimen. The creatures live deep in the ocean, so it seemed impossible to capture—or even photograph—one.

Dr. Clyde Roper wanted to change that. He is a marine **biologist** at the Smithsonian Institution who became obsessed with the giant squid in the 1960s. Roper was frustrated by how little was known about the creature. "We probably know more about dinosaurs than we do about the giant squid," he often said.

Roper's dream was to film a living giant squid in its natural **habitat**. But the ocean is huge, so his first challenge was figuring out where to look.

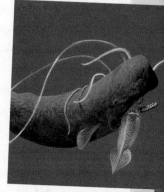

Whalers often found pieces of giant squid in the stomachs of sperm whales. They could tell that the battles between the two giants were fierce. The squid's suckers left deep scars on the whales' skin.

# The Squid Squad

**Roper's team set out to film giant squid—with a little help from sperm whales.**

Roper knew that sperm whales eat giant squid. So he decided to focus his search on places where those whales gather. After choosing several locations, he and his group—which he called the squid squad—set out on their search.

43

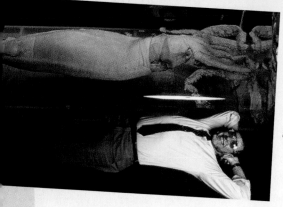

Squid-hunter Dr. Clyde Roper stretches out near a fairly small giant squid. This specimen is only about nine feet (3m) long.

Between 1996 and 1999, Roper led three squid-hunting expeditions. The team mounted cameras on small manned and unmanned submarines. They lowered cameras on long lines that had bait on them. And they put cameras on the backs of sperm whales.

That's right. The camera crew included whales. Roper's team stuck crittercams—cameras carried by creatures—on the backs of eight sperm whales. The hope was that the whales would hunt some giant squid while carrying the cameras. However, none of the crittercam-wearing whales managed to film a giant squid.

This dolphin has been fitted with a crittercam. It allows scientists to see what the animal sees.

The human cameramen's luck was no better. Roper was very disappointed. Still, the crew caught many other amazing deep-sea creatures on film. And Roper was pleased that media coverage of the expeditions taught people about the giant squid, a "mysterious, wonderful, and real monster."

# Snagging a Squid

**After many failed expeditions, scientists finally capture a live giant squid on film.**

The giant squid got even more press attention in 2004. A scientist named Tsunemi Kubodera finally did what nobody had done before: he snapped a photo of a live giant squid. In fact, he snapped hundreds of them.

Kubodera works at the National Science Museum in Tokyo, Japan. That year, he and his team were working near the Ogasawara Islands south of Japan. On September 30, the scientists lowered a camera attached to a baited fishing line to a depth of 2,950 feet (900 m). There's no light that deep in the ocean, so the camera had lights attached to it. Kubodera hoped the bait—a small squid—would attract a giant squid to the camera.

The plan worked. A giant squid suddenly appeared and began attacking the bait. It was very aggressive, using "its tentacles to strike and tangle the prey," as Kubodera told reporters. After a while, one of the tentacles got snagged on the hook. As the giant squid struggled to free itself, the camera clicked away.

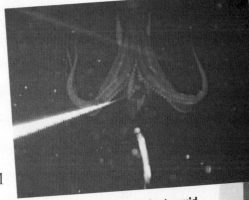

Here, a giant squid attacks a baited line. This image was captured by Tsunemi Kudobera, the first person to photograph a live giant squid.

Kudobera examines a squid's tentacle, which broke off when the animal escaped. "It was quite an experience to feel the still-functioning tentacle in my hand," he told the Associated Press.

The team got more than 500 pictures before the giant squid's tentacle broke off and the animal swam away. The researchers reeled the tentacle in. It was 18 feet (5.5 m) long. Kubodera was surprised when its suckers gripped his hand.

Scientists are pleased that the giant squid has finally been captured on film. But they still have many questions about the animal. Nobody knows how long it lives, for instance, or how fast it grows. This big monster remains a big mystery. 24/7

# EYE TO EYE WITH A GIANT SQUID

**Kubodera was also the first person to film this creature.**

In 2006, Kubodera caught another giant squid. The team filmed it as they pulled it to the surface. It was the first video ever taken of the animal. The squid—a young female—"put up quite a fight," Kubodera said. This photo shows the squid just as it reached the surface. It was the first time anyone had ever looked into the eyes of a giant squid.

Does the fact that it's so hard to find giant squid mean that there are only a few of them? Kubodera doesn't think so. He estimates that there are 200,000 sperm whales, and each one eats up to a ton of food every day. "That would suggest that there are quite a few giant squid for them to be feeding on," he told the Web site UnderwaterTimes.com.

# CRYPTID DOWNLOAD

Have you ever heard of living fossils? Or have you wondered what it's like to be a cryptozoologist?

# 1

### Third century BC
### The Wildman of China

Chinese poet Qu Yuan writes a poem about a mountain monster. It is the earliest written record of a Bigfoot-like creature. There are many other mentions of a "man bear" or "hairy man" in later Chinese historical documents. Sightings of the creature, which is known as the Yeren or Wildman, are still being reported.

# Key Dates in Cryptozoology

**People have been seeing mysterious creatures for a long time.**

# 2

### AD 1861 Battling a Monster

Sailors on the French gunboat *Alecton* try to capture a giant squid. They fire at it with guns and cannons. Few people believe their story. But Jules Verne uses it as the basis for a scene in *20,000 Leagues Under the Sea*. In this book, sailors battle several giant squid. (This illustration is from the original 1870 edition of the book.)

See Case #3.

### 1920s Sasquatch Is Born

J. W. Burns, a teacher working in Canada, collects Native American stories about a wild, hairy beast living in the woods. Some of the legends go back hundreds of years. Burns combines several Indian names for the creature and creates the word "Sasquatch." Today, the terms *Sasquatch* and *Bigfoot* refer to the same cryptid.

See Case #1.

## BEWARE OF SASQUATCH

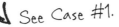

### 1935 Naming Nessie

John and Aldie Mackay report that they spotted an "enormous animal" in a Scottish lake. The local paper calls it the Loch Ness Monster, and the name sticks.

See Case #2.

### 1938 Catch of the Century

A South African fisherman nets a huge fish called a coelacanth. Scientists had previously found only **fossils** of the fish. That had led them to conclude that the species became extinct 65 million years ago. Often called a "living fossil," the coelacanth gives cryptozoologists hope that other animals considered extinct could still be found.

### 1967 The Bigfoot Craze Begins

Roger Patterson shoots a film of Bigfoot. Since then, many people have become fascinated with cryptids. But today, after decades of research, most of these creatures remain as mysterious as ever.

49

# The Funny Pages

## Do you know the one about Bigfoot and Nessie?

You'll probably never spot a Bigfoot or the Loch Ness Monster in the wild. But there's no way you'll miss seeing these creatures in popular culture. There's a monster truck called Bigfoot, a Bigfoot action figure, Loch Ness Monster stuffed animals, a Loch Ness roller coaster. . . .

The monsters also show up in newspapers—especially the kind you find in the grocery store. According to one story, Bigfoot is from another dimension. Another story claims that Nessie was kidnapped by aliens. No wonder people haven't seen the creature for a while!

The big hairy guy and the long-necked beauty also appear in cartoons. Here's a look at a few of them.

"IT LOOKS TO ME AS THOUGH THE YETI'S INTO LINE DANCING".

"Do you believe in Bigfoot?"

"I GIVE UP. WHAT IS NINE FEET TALL AND HAS TWO FANGS AND HAS HAIR ALL OVER ITS BODY?"

# HELP WANTED:
# Primatologist

You'll never see job listings for a cryptozoologists. They earn their living in other fields. Here's an interview with a primatologist— an expert on apes—who is also a leading Bigfoot researcher.

Dr. Jeffrey Meldrum is a professor of anatomy and primatology.

## Q&A: DR. JEFFREY MELDRUM

**24/7: How did you get interested in studying Bigfoot?**

**DR. JEFFREY MELDRUM:** [I knew that Bigfoot researchers Grover Krantz and Paul Freeman had] been collecting casts of footprints for many years. As a **primatologist**, I study how the foot bends and moves when a two-legged animal walks. The way an ape walks is different from the way a human walks.

**24/7: How does studying the way apes and humans walk help your research on Bigfoot?**

**DR. MELDRUM:** [Say you have a plaster cast of] an extremely large footprint. And you learn that it was made by an animal that doesn't walk like a human. That provides strong evidence that the track was made by [a two-legged ape-like creature] such as Sasquatch.
[Note: Scientists often use the word "Sasquatch" rather than "Bigfoot."]

**24/7: What was your first experience with Sasquatch?**

**DR. MELDRUM:** In 1996, I went to visit Paul Freeman and saw his collection of casts. Then he showed me some fresh tracks [in the woods]. I made some plaster casts of these tracks and began my own collection and study.

**24/7:** **Did you need any special training to become a Sasquatch researcher?**

**DR. MELDRUM:** My own study of anthropology and primatology was a natural lead-in to investigating the existence of these creatures.

**24/7:** **Describe a typical day investigating tracks.**

**DR. MELDRUM:** [When I find some tracks, first I try to] rule out any chance of a hoax. Then, [I fill the tracks with plaster to] make a cast. [I take that cast] back to my lab. I also try to interview any local witnesses who claim to have seen the animal that made the tracks.

## THE STATS

**DAY JOB:** Some cryptozoologists are scientists and college professors. Others make their living as writers, teachers, wilderness guides, or in other ways. For many people, searching for unknown species is a hobby.

**MONEY:** The average income for a full-time college faculty member is about $70,000. Some people make money writing about cryptozoology, or by organizing research expeditions. But for most, working in this field is a labor of love.

**EDUCATION:** Cryptozoologists need to have a good understanding of zoology and other sciences. So it's necessary to take college-level science courses.

**24/7:** **What's your favorite thing about your job?**

**DR. MELDRUM:** Working on the forefront of what could be the discovery of a previously unknown species on Earth.

**24/7:** **What advice do you have for young people interested in this subject?**

**DR. MELDRUM:** Study as much about anthropology and animal biology as you can. You need a solid basic knowledge about animals we do know exist (like apes), if you are trying to discover the existence of new species. Also, don't let the skeptics discourage you from your investigations. But always be careful of hoaxes.

# DO YOU HAVE WHAT IT TAKES?

**Take this totally unscientific quiz to see if you have what it takes to be a cryptozoologist.**

**1** **Do you like learning about animals?**
- a) My favorite channel is Animal Planet.
- b) I like going to the zoo, but reading about animals gets boring.
- c) The only animals I'm interested in are my goldfish.

**2** **Do you enjoy being in the woods?**
- a) I like the idea of getting lost in the woods and sleeping out under the stars.
- b) The woods are okay, but I don't like all the bugs.
- c) I avoid places where bears live.

**3** **Are you curious about the unknown?**
- a) Who doesn't want to find out if the Tasmanian tiger is really extinct?
- b) I'm only curious about things that affect me directly.
- c) I'm pretty sure I already know everything.

**4** **Do you enjoy solving mysteries?**
- a) I love figuring things out.
- b) I like reading mysteries, but solving them sounds like a lot of work.
- c) I get frustrated when I don't know exactly what's going on.

**5** **Do you have a lot of patience?**
- a) Yes. I enjoy the suspense of looking forward to something.
- b) I guess. But waiting for things can be a drag.
- c) No. Next question?

## YOUR SCORE

Give yourself 3 points for every "**a**" you chose.
Give yourself 2 points for every "**b**" you chose.
Give yourself 1 point for every "**c**" you chose.

If you got **13–15 points**, you should consider a career in zoology. Then you'll have the skills you need to study unknown species.

If you got **10–12 points**, you might want to think about a career in science.

If you got **5–9 points**, your career should not involve mysteries of any kind.

1
2
3
4
5
6
7
8
9
10

# HOW TO GET STARTED...NOW!

## GET AN EDUCATION

▶ Focus on your science classes, especially biology.

▶ Start thinking about college. Look for ones with good science programs. You'll want to go to a college that offers courses in zoology, anatomy, anthropology, and wildlife biology.

▶ Read anything you can find about cryptozoology, and also about animals in general. See the books and Web sites in the Resources section on pages 56–58.

▶ Graduate from high school!

## NETWORK!

▶ Find out about cryptozoology organizations in your area.

▶ Look for zoologists or wildlife biologists in your community whom you can talk to about your interest in animals and mysterious species.

## GET AN INTERNSHIP

Look for internships that involve working with animals. Ask about opportunities at your local zoo or at a veterinarian's office.

**It's never too early to start working toward your goals.**

## LEARN ABOUT JOBS IN THE FIELD

These are some of the jobs held by people interested in cryptozoology:

▶ anthropologist
▶ filmmaker
▶ journalist
▶ park ranger
▶ photographer
▶ primatologist
▶ wilderness guide
▶ wildlife biologist
▶ zoologist

**A cast of a Bigfoot footprint?**

55

# Resources

Looking for more information about cryptozoology?
Here are some resources you don't want to miss!

## WEB SITES

### The Committee for Skeptical Inquiry
www.csicop.org

This international organization supports and encourages the scientific investigation of claims about mysterious and paranormal events. Its goal is to expose fake science and to promote critical thinking and scientific inquiry.

### Cryptomundo.com
www.cryptomundo.com

This site has up-to-date news on things happening in the world of cryptozoology. It includes blogs written by some leading cryptozoologists.

### Cryptozoology.com
www.cryptozoology.com

The Web site is a place where people post articles and share opinions about all aspects of cryptozoology.

### Pibburns.com
www.pibburns.com/cryptozo.htm

There are many cryptozoology sites, and this one provides links to many of the best ones.

### Lorencoleman.com
www.lorencoleman.com

The Web site of one of the world's leading cryptozoologists, Loren Coleman. He has written many books and articles on cryptids of all kinds.

### The Loch Ness Project
www.lochnessproject.org

A site filled with scientific information about Loch Ness and the search for Nessie.

## Loch Ness Investigation
www.lochnessinvestigation.org

This site was created by a longtime Nessie researcher and includes lots of historical information about the investigations into the Loch Ness Monster.

## The Smithsonian Institution National Museum of Natural History
http://seawifs.gsfc.nasa.gov/squid.html

This Smithsonian Web site is an online exhibition that answers all your questions about the giant squid.

## Bigfoot Field Researchers Organization
www.bfro.net

This nationwide organization of researchers is dedicated to sharing information about Bigfoot sightings and research.

## Bigfoot Encounters
www.bigfootencounters.com

Check out this site to read about people's Bigfoot sightings.

## Orgeonbigfoot.com
www.oregonbigfoot.com

This Web site has photos, videos, and audio recordings of Bigfoot. It's up to visitors to decide whether they are real or not.

## Floridaskunkape.com
www.floridaskunkape.com

This site has information about the Florida Skunk Ape as well as an updated list of sightings.

# BOOKS

Coleman, Loren. *Bigfoot! The True Story of Apes in America.* New York: Paraview Pocket Books, 2003.

Coleman, Loren, and Jerome Clark. *Cryptozoology from A to Z: The Encyclopedia Of Loch Monsters, Sasquatch, Chupacabras, and Other Authentic Mysteries of Nature.* New York: Fireside, 1999.

Coleman, Loren, and Patrick Huyghe. *The Field Guide to Bigfoot, Yeti, and Other Mystery Primates Worldwide.* New York: Avon Books, 1999.

Coleman, Loren, and Patrick Huyghe. *The Field Guide to Lake Monsters, Sea Serpents, and Other Mystery Denizens of the Deep.* New York: Tarcher, 2003.

Owens, L. L. *Bigfoot: The Legend Lives On.* Logan, Iowa: Perfection Learning, 1999.

Thome, Ian. *Bigfoot: Search for the Unknown.* Parsippany, N.J.: Crestwood House, 1978.

Yorke, Malcolm. *Beastly Tales: Yeti, Bigfoot, and the Loch Ness Monster.* New York: DK Publishing, 1999.

# DVDS

*Ancient Mysteries: Bigfoot.* A&E DVD Archives, 1994.

*Rocky Mountain Bigfoot.* BT Media, 2004.

# A

**anatomy** (uh-NAT-uh-mee) *noun* the scientific study of the structure of living things

**anthropology** (AN-thruh-POL-uh-jee) *noun* the study of the customs, social structure, and institutions of humans. This also includes the myths and legends of humans.

# B

**biologist** (bye-OL-uh-jist) *noun* a scientist who studies animals and their environments

# C

**chimpanzees** (chim-pan-ZEEZ) *noun* small apes with dark fur that come from Africa

**credible** (KRED-uh-buhl) *adjective* believable; capable of being believed

**crittercams** (KRIT-ur-kamz) *noun* video cameras that researchers attach to animals. Crittercams let people see an animal's world from its point of view.

**cryptid** (KRIP-tid) *noun* a creature that some people believe is real but whose existence has not been scientifically proven

**cryptozoologists** (KRIP-toh-zoh-OL-uh-jists) *noun* scientists who study animals that may or may not exist. This includes animals from myths or legends.

**cryptozoology** (KRIP-toh-zoh-OL-uh-jee) *noun* the study of hidden, unknown, or yet-to-be-discovered animals

**currents** (KUR-ents) *noun* the movements of water in a river or an ocean

# D

**determined** (di-TUR-mind) *adjective* feeling or showing firmness or a fixed purpose

# E

**enormous** (ih-NOR-muhss) *adjective* extremely large

**evidence** (EV-uh-denss) *noun* information and objects that help people make judgments or come to conclusions

**expeditions** (ek-spuh-DISH-uhnz) *noun* long journeys for a special purpose, such as exploring

Dictionary

# F

**fibbing** (FIB-ing) *verb* telling an insignificant, harmless, or small lie

**fossils** (FOSS-uhls) *noun* hardened remains of plants or animals

# G

**Gigantopithecus blacki** (jye-GAN-TOH-pith-uh-kuss BLA-kye) *noun* scientific name given to a species of giant ape believed to exist by Dutch scientist Ralph von Koenigswald in 1954

# H

**habitat** (HAB-uh-tat) *noun* home environment

**hoax** (hohks) *noun* an act or trick designed to fool people into believing something that isn't true

# I

**inconclusive** (in-kuhn-KLOO-siv) *adjective* not clear, or not certain

**invertebrate** (in-VUR-tuh-brit) *noun* a creature without a backbone

# L

**legends** (LEJ-uhndz) *noun* stories that have been passed down for generations, especially ones that are presented as history but are unlikely to be true

# M

**mammal** (MAM-uhl) *noun* an animal that is warm blooded, has a backbone, and whose females produce milk to feed their young

**mythical creature** (MITH-i-kuhl KREE-chur) *noun* a fantastical animal that exists only in legends and folktales

# P

**plaster cast** (PLASS-tuhr KAST) *noun* a model created by pouring plaster into a given shape and allowing it to harden

**predator** (PRED-uh-tur) *noun* an animal that lives by hunting other animals for food

**primates** (PRYE-maytss) *noun* members of the group of animals that includes humans, apes, monkeys, and chimpanzees

**primatologist** (PRY-muh-TOL-uh-jist) *noun* a scientist who studies primates

# S

**sacrifices** (SAH-kruh-fyse-ez) *noun* offerings to honor or make peace with a god; these offerings may be slaughtered animals, or even humans

**sightings** (SYE-tings) *noun* catching sight of something, especially something unusual or unexpected

**skeptic** (SKEP-tik) *noun* someone who questions ideas, beliefs, or evidence

**sonar** (SOH-nar) *noun* equipment that sends out sound waves. When the waves strike an object, they return and create an image of the object on a video screen.

**species** (SPEE-sheez) *noun* a group of organisms that share specific characteristics and can mate to produce offspring

# T

**tentacles** (TEN-tuh-kuhlz) *noun* long, flexible limbs of some animals, such as the octopus or squid. Tentacles are used for moving, feeling, and grasping.

# U

**urban myth** (UR-buhn mith) *noun* a strangely believable but untrue story that many people believe. Like rumors, urban myths spread fast.

# Z

**zoologist** (zoh-AH-luh-jist) *noun* a scientist who studies and classifies animals

# Index

**W**hile writing this book, I was surprised to learn that up until 1847, people didn't know that gorillas existed. And that up until 1902, the same was true about the mountain gorilla. I also thought that Bigfoot was a myth. But after doing research for this book, I understand why cryptozoologists think that Sasquatch may well be the next large ape waiting to be discovered.

I learned that far more people believe in the Loch Ness Monster than I would have thought, even though so little evidence has been found. And I was thrilled to discover the tales of the giant squid as it moved from merely a creature of legend (like Bigfoot and Nessie) to a real live creature caught on film.

If you'd like to know more, check out the Resources section in this book. You can also Google *Bigfoot, Loch Ness Monster,* and *giant squid* to find lots of great Web sites about these creatures.

I'd like to thank Dr. Jeffrey Meldrum of Idaho State University for sharing his papers, his time on the phone, and his great knowledge. Having access to a serious scholar in this field made all the difference in the writing of this book.

**CONTENT ADVISER:** Loren Coleman, International Cryptozoology Museum